Alex is Mr. Jolly
Sharing Happiness

written by
Lynn C. Skinner

illustrated by
Ingrid Dohm

Alex is Mr. Jolly
Copyright © 2020 by Lynn C. Skinner. All rights reserved.

No part of this publication may be reproduced, stored in a retrieval system or transmitted in any way by any means, electronic, mechanical, photocopy, recording or otherwise without the prior permission of the author except as provided by USA copyright law.

Published by Lynn C. Skinner
PO Box 34 | Alley, Georgia 30410 USA
Cover and Layout Design by Christina Hicks Creative

Published in the United States of America
softcover isbn: 978-1-7336531-4-5
ebook isbn: 978-1-7336531-5-2

This book belongs to:

_____

ACKNOWLEDGMENT

Our thanks to Alex and his parents for allowing us to share this story. The illustrator and I dedicate this book to them and their positive choices.

Beep, beep went the bicycle horn. "Oh, oh" laughed the two farmers at the garden fence. "Here comes Alex and he is always so happy."

As Alex approaches, pedaling his special bicycle with his arms, the other neighbor replies, "Yes and he always smiles."

Alex was born in the country of Russia. When he was young, he was placed in an orphanage. The caregivers noticed a problem with his bones.

When he was about 8 years old, he was sent from Russia to the United States of America for surgery on his legs.

For a young person who could speak only Russian, this should have been difficult. He might have been scared but Alex smiled. He understood that strangers were trying to help him and the nurses and doctors in America were kind to Alex.

As he recovered from his operation, an American family with seven children and a huge St. Bernard dog, Heidi, decided to adopt Alex.

This was so different for Alex. He enjoyed having many siblings to play with him and Heidi, the dog, was fun but Alex had to learn the English language. He also had to learn to read English and complete his schoolwork in English. Alex learned quickly.

There were good times too like sledding with his brothers and sisters in the snow. The snow reminded him of Russia.

There were games to be played and new foods to taste and chores to be done.

The years passed quickly and soon Alex wanted to learn to drive. His father talked to the Department of Transportation and developed a way for him to drive with a special car. Alex especially liked to roll down the window and wave.

Even though Alex had to sit in a wheelchair, he graduated from school and rolled himself across the stage to receive his diploma.

How is Alex now? He has learned a new language, learned American ways and learned to live with his bone problems. He has continued to smile. He even enjoys riding bicycles with his parents.

What is Alex doing now? He has discovered that he enjoys repairing computers and cell phones and helping friends with technical problems.

Even though Alex will always have challenges with his bones, Alex chooses to be happy. He laughs, he waves, he smiles, he nods a greeting and shares happiness with those he meets. What about you? Have you shared any happiness today?

ABOUT THE AUTHOR

Writing about people who choose to smile is a pleasure. We all have challenges in life – some large, some small, some permanent, some temporary but each of us must live through our situations. Whether we choose to be angry and sad or positive and happy is the decision. Alex is a real person who is friendly, helpful and engaging. This is his story of personal decisions.

ABOUT THE ILLUSTRATOR

In this second book in the Sharing Happiness series, the illustrations have a Russian or European influence in honor of Alex's birth country and my birth country of Austria. Painting is a joy and reflects my own happiness. As a wife, mother, grandmother and artist, it is a pleasure to show Alex's choice to be happy with my paint brush.

www.ingramcontent.com/pod-product-compliance
Lightning Source LLC
Chambersburg PA
CBHW061226070526
44584CB00029B/4005